KAIZEN

An Easy Introduction

Author

Harry Altman

© Copyright 2018 - All rights reserved.

If you would like to share this book with another person, please purchase an additional copy for each recipient. Thank you for respecting the hard work of this author. Otherwise, the transmission, duplication or reproduction of any of the following work including specific information will be considered an illegal act irrespective of if it is done electronically or in print. This extends to creating a secondary or tertiary copy of the work or a recorded copy and is only allowed with an express written consent from the Publisher. All additional right reserved.

TABLE OF CONTENTS

INTRODUCTION 5

CHAPTER 1 13
THE HISTORY OF KAIZEN AND ITS EFFECT ON THE REAL WORLD 13

CHAPTER 2 19
DIFFERENT TYPES OF KAIZEN 19
    POINT KAIZEN 19
    SYSTEM KAIZEN 20
    LINE KAIZEN 21
    PLANE KAIZEN 21
    CUBE KAIZEN 21

CHAPTER 3 23
10 STEPS TO SUCCESS WITH KAIZEN 23

CHAPTER 4 31
HOW TO CREATE A KAIZEN CULTURE AT HOME AND AT WORK 31

CHAPTER 5 41
KAIZEN METHODS & BENEFITS 41

CHAPTER 6 44
PERSONAL KAIZEN 44

CONCLUSION 48

INTRODUCTION

To be cheerful, to make others happy, to live life to its fullest... these are the main aspects of our lives we ceaselessly try to enhance throughout our everyday life. Without joy and seeing the grinning faces of those around us, what kind of life would we live?

Today, I want to acquaint you with something that many refer to as kaizen – a large number of you may have known about this previously, however, to a few this might be a foreign word.

Kaizen is a Japanese administration technique that can be fused into all aspects of your life, from work circumstances to individual life issues, and the administration thereof.

Generally interpreted, it signifies a "Consistent moderate change, or great change."

So, what the hell is Kaizen?

Kaizen is a rationality with birthplaces in Japan, which is making incremental strides towards enhancing business procedures, items, and quality. It can be characterized as a ceaseless exertion by all representatives of the association to guarantee nonstop change of the considerable number of procedures and frameworks within the association. It subsequently helps in killing waste from the association. It can likewise be connected to forms, such as buying and coordinations, which cross authoritative limits into the store's network.

The Kaizen process goes for a persistent change of procedures and quality and in this days and age, it has been connected to various fields like social insurance, government, funding, programming, and several other enterprises.

Kaizen is the logic of utilizing little advances, or commitments, that work towards a major change, or the "big picture." It centers around you and me, the people that shape some portion of a private company, partnership, or even a nation. It includes the seemingly insignificant details that can be changed by every last one of us, on the way to winding up better, more beneficial, and fitter human beings.

This is accomplished by focusing and enhancing the easily overlooked details that with time, exertion, and consistency indicate a lifestyle that makes achievements easily. To get to this point, we need to vanquish our terrible dietary patterns, meditating, absence of action, and stress.

We need to take little (however relentless) strides towards accomplishing our objectives, regardless of what they may be! We can utilize the power and adequacy of Kaizen to achieve the greater part of this.

Kaizen is a long-haul idea. It takes a long-haul perspective and the most essential standards that are every day, nonstop, and enduring activities. It isn't critical that gigantic and sudden improvements are made. Little enhancements are incredible and it is imperative that you constantly take a gander at the methods for improving things, regardless of how little they are. You know the expression, "On the off chance that it works, why change it?" Well, the Kaizen reasoning proposes that there are dependable approaches to enhance things, regardless of how small these progressions might be.

How is Kaizen actualized?

Kaizen exercises are normally actualized by utilizing the Plan-Do-Check-Act (PDCA) cycle. This guarantees that there is an on-going cycle in real life to screen changes and improvements upon them.

Plan - Define the issue and create potential arrangements. The required goals and procedures are set and data is accumulated that is expected to gain the normal yield.

Do – Implement the arrangement and execute the set procedures. Gather information, assuming any, to be utilized as a part of the consequent stages.

Check – Evaluate results to check whether the arrangement fulfilled the normal results. Look for any deviations in usage from the arrangement. Change the acquired information into data.

Act – Based on the data, if things are going admirably according to the arrangement, at that point take measures to balance out the progressions or something else, rehash the PDCA cycle if there are still some uncertain issues.

How does Kaizen function?

Kaizen works by diminishing waste (muda) and wiping out work forms that are excessively troublesome (muri). It succeeds when workers at all the levels of the association order search for enhancements and give their proposals and input in light of their experience and perceptions. By and large, these proposals are about little changes that can be made to existing business forms that can give positive outcomes to the business over a drawn-out period of time. For this to work, it is critical that it is clarified that any sorts of recommendations from anybody are welcome and there would be no negative effects for cooperation. Rather, the representatives will be compensated for supporting the everyday exercises.

Kaizen's 5 essential components

Kaizen is established upon five essential components:

Quality Circles: A quality circle is a gathering of individuals who chip away at the same or comparative task, who meet all the time to distinguish, break down, and comprehend work-related issues, assuming there are any.

Enhanced Morale: It is a critical advancement in accomplishing long-haul effectiveness and efficiency.

Cooperation: Kaizen enables representatives to feel that all are a member of the group and need to put in aggregate endeavors so they can succeed.

Individual Discipline: A pledge of individual work ethics by every worker guarantees that the group will remain solid.

Proposals for Improvement: Gathering criticism from every one of the workers guarantees that all issues are tended to before they turn out to be enormous.

We as a whole realize that it is smarter to prevent an issue than to settle one. By fusing Kaizen standards into your life, any snag to your prosperity can be evacuated, regardless of whether or not it is with extra special care. Simply recall the fact a thousand-mile walk starts with the initial step.

How to begin?

You need to begin with your brain. What spurs you? What is your purpose behind needing to do whatever it is you need to do, be it weight reduction, arranging a trek, or enhancing your money-related prosperity? In what manner will achieving those objectives influence you to feel and how it may change your life?

We need to figure out how to be understanding. This must be estimated by your sense of duty regarding your objectives. You are resolving to make changes to enhance your life and this won't change overnight. As it's been said many times before, "Rome was not built in a day!"

When you have grasped Kaizen logic, you won't be put off by mishaps, however, you will improve your vision with your goals in clear view.

Now is a great opportunity to investigate the subject of Kaizen, and through this short trip we will reveal precisely what kaizen is, the history behind it, the distinctive types of Kaizen, how to make a Kaizen domain in your home, and so much more.

Chapter 1

The History Of Kaizen And Its Effect On The Real World

After World War II had ended, the American occupation powers were asked to allow Japan to recuperate from the brutal outcomes of the war that the nation experienced. In a joint effort with Japanese business officials, this group formed new measures to enhance business procedures, quality, and efficiency.

In the meantime, the Civil Communications Section (CCS) chipped away at building up an administration that prepared programs which tried to educate people about measurable control strategies. Homer Sarasohn and Charles Protzman created this course amid 1949-1950. Sarasohn prescribed W. Edwards Deming for additional preparation.

The Economic and Scientific Section (ESS) was additionally doled out with the errand of enhancing Japanese administrative aptitudes, and Edgar McVoy conveyed Lowell Mellen to Japan to help in building up the Training Within Industry (TWI) programs in 1951.

Prior to the landing of Mellen in 1951, the ESS assembly showed a preparation film about the TWI 3J standards Job Instruction, Job Methods, and Job Relations. This film was titled "Change in Four Stages." This was Japan's first acquaintance with Kaizen.

In 1960, the Emperor of Japan granted the second request of awarding the Medal of the Sacred Treasure to Dr. Deming for presenting, spearheading, and executing Kaizen in Japan.

Kaizen was first received by Toyota when it executed quality circles in its creation procedure. A quality circle is a gathering of individuals who deal with the same or comparative task, who meet all the time to recognize, break down, and understand business-related issues.

This prompted the arrangement of the Toyota Production System, driven by Taiichi Ohno, a previous Executive Vice-President of Toyota Motor Company. This expected to make an arrangement of constant change in quality, forms, profitability, administration, and innovation. This idea soon became mainstream and added to the nation's prosperity on the worldwide market.

In 1986, Masaaki Imai's acquainted Kaizen with whatever is left of the world through one of his top of the line books, called "Kaizen: The Key to Japan's Competitive Success."

Effect of Kaizen in reality

Kaizen is a logic that can be connected to all circles of our lives, be it our working, social, or home life. The usage of Kaizen suggests that there is a dependable scope for development and one ought not be totally happy with one's past accomplishments, so you must always try to improve upon them.

At the point when organizations begin to apply the idea of Kaizen, it points towards enhancements in the general population, items, and the procedures followed in a given organization. Representatives who are best at their occupations recommend changes that would help in settling issues rapidly and effectively. These progressions are then imparted to everybody in the group with the goal that whatever remains of the group can likewise begin applying Kaizen.

An investigation of 236 workers from three distinct offices has demonstrated that the selection of Kaizen has prompted work advancement and an ascent in inspiration. Employment fulfillment likewise prompts fulfillment in one's own life, thus enhancing lives in individual and work circles.

Kaizen has numerous advantages, some of which are shown below.

The procedure of Kaizen helps guarantee that any obstructions or dangers to the task are recognized in the underlying phases of the undertaking and illuminated promptly.

It intends to decrease the misuse of an association by a powerful administration. Since this technique empowers those to constantly improve, workers are requested to lead meetings to generate new ideas to concoct new and imaginative plans to diminish squander. This additionally guarantees that individuals who work in a group achieve a positive result.

Organizations who actualize Kaizen are skilled at process-arranged reasoning, implying that the strategy for accomplishing a specific outcome is as imperative as the outcome itself.

Kaizen has turned out to be monstrously fruitful in Japanese business, and it is capable of giving Japan the cutting edge in the worldwide market. In view of such accomplishments, this theory is currently being intensely actualized in associations from different parts of the world. Since it centers around change, it has extraordinary positive effects to the organizations and furthermore in different circles of life.

Chapter 2

Different Types Of Kaizen

Kaizen, if executed in an association, is the duty of the considerable number of representatives and not only a couple of choice individuals.

There are diverse manners by which the Kaizen rationality can be executed in the working environment, some of which are shown below.

Point Kaizen

It is a standout amongst the most generally executed sorts of Kaizen. It happens rapidly and generally without much arranging. When something is discovered to be broken or off base, quick measures are taken to address the issues.

These measures are, for the most part, small and simple to execute, but they can have a tremendous effect.

Now and again it is likewise conceivable that the constructive outcomes of Point Kaizen in one region can lessen or dispose of advantages of Point Kaizen in some other region. A case of Point Kaizen could be a shop investigation by a chief where he finds broken materials or other little issues, and after that he solicits the proprietor from the shop to play out a snappy Kaizen (5S) to correct these issues.

System Kaizen

System Kaizen is formulated to address framework-level issues in an association.

It is an upper level, vital arrangement technique that brings out various arranged Kaizen occasions over a long period of time. It is different than Point Kaizen which happens as a result of identification of a small issue which is settled in a brief timeframe.

Line Kaizen

"Line" in this context refers to an organized spread of Lean from a point to the line. For instance, Kaizen may be connected to a procedure (point), yet additionally to the downstream procedure. Those two points constitute a Line Kaizen.

Plane Kaizen

It is following the upper level of Line Kaizen, in that a few lines are associated together. This can likewise be portrayed as an value stream, where rather than conventional offices, the association is organized into product offerings or families and value streams. It can be envisioned as changes or upgrades made to one line being actualized to numerous different lines or procedures.

Cube Kaizen

Cube Kaizen portrays the circumstance where every one of the purposes of the planes are associated with each other and no point is disconnected from each other. This would look like a circumstance where Lean has spread over the whole association. Upgrades are made all over the plane, upstream, or downstream, including the entire association, providers, and clients. This may require a few changes in the standard business forms as well.

Chapter 3

10 Steps to Success With Kaizen

Mr. Masaaki Imai is the main individual to acquaint Kaizen with the world outside of Japan. He utilized his book, "Kaizen, the Key to Japan's Competitive Success," keeping the end goal in mind to help get the message out.

We will now take a look at the 10 steps of progressing with the Kaizen specialty of persistent change.

Stage One: Continue learning

To begin, it is essential that you understand that Kaizen is eccentric. This implies that it isn't important to keep adapting all our lives through.

Subsequently, the fundamental thought is to understand that as you go about your everyday life, you ought to continue learning on the grounds that new and innovational thoughts are consistently flying up around each corner ... the world keeps on developing, thus so should your psyche.

Stage Two: Continue pondering how YOU can accomplish something

Individuals tend to focus on the negative – are you a casualty of "negative reasoning?" Instead of concentrating on the things you are not ready to do, what you ought to do at the present time is concentrating your psyche on those things you can do. This is called being a hopeful forward mastermind. Proceed this way and before you know it, you'll be achieving something new that you never thought conceivable.

Continuously keep your psyche forward and centered around the results, and discover ways where the results CAN be proficient.

Stage Three: Eliminate those excuses

"I didn't do this in light of the fact that… " stop that in its tracks – quit rationalizing. Coming up with pardons is the greatest rationalization in the book to not accomplish something. Begin looking for answers to current practices by making inquiries. Spotlight the result and after that can you begin to make a move. In the event that you keep on trying, you won't stall out – you will ceaselessly go in a forward movement.

Stage Four: Never surrender and never strive for perfection

"Surrendering" shouldn't be in your vocabulary. Surrendering is disappointment and that isn't adequate. On a similar level, you should never take a stab at flawlessness. When you have achieved something up to a specific point don't simply leave, rather keep at it until the point where you have finished everything the way. Sure, there might be issues en route, however you can make changes as you go.

Stage Five: Fix the mistakes

As you're accomplishing something, botches are presumably going to fly up in unforeseen circumstances. In the event that this happens, don't continue onward.

Instead, discover the answer for the mix-up. Discover where you turned out badly so you can maintain a strategic distance from that error the second time. It's implied that "we gain from our own missteps." If the error includes other individuals, all you can do is adjust accordingly as fast and as best as you can.

Stage Six: Don't disregard your knowledge

Don't simply burn through cash for Kaizen; you ought to likewise be utilizing your knowledge. The way to this is activity? Begin by picking up all that you have to know, and at that point make a move in view of what you have realized.

Stage Seven: Challenges are learning opportunities

Everybody has their own difficulties that they need to traverse throughout their everyday lives. At the point when a test strolls in your way, you ought to remember it as a learning opportunity.

Truly, on the off chance that we didn't have these difficulties, we presumably wouldn't learn as much as we are aware of today. Deterrents will fly up most wherever and when you wouldn't dare hoping anymore. Simply recall the fact that all you do will improve you turn into a responsible adult. Bounce over those obstacles, figure out how to defeat them and be remunerated for those activities at last. After one test leaves another test may fly up before you, so be ready to hop over that one too.

Stage Eight: Don't be reluctant to ask "Why"

Such a large number of individuals fear the question "why." Does that sound like you? Quit being apprehensive, there is nothing amiss when inquiring as to why.

By asking the why, you will have the capacity to find what the base of the undertaking is that you need to achieve – it will enable you to comprehend it better. By understanding why something should be done, your odds of finishing the assignment all the way will increase tremendously.

Stage Nine: Group belief is something worth being thankful for

Gathering belief is something that you should consider. As we would see it, it is constantly better to look for the insight of ten individuals than the learning of one. There is a gigantic measure of energy in "gather considering."

This could include holding a gathering with a meeting of individuals to conceptualize together – this is the way things get finished. It is smarter to talk about an assignment with a gathering of individuals as this will build up the odds of the task completing itself the correct way – in the event that you are finding the solutions from one individual that may not know how things are done, your odds of coming up short will also increase.

Along these lines, because of those contemplations, it is vital that you make sure to ask how something is done from individuals who have effectively experienced the procedure and finished – don't be hesitant to approach a gathering for assistance with an assignment that needs finishing.

Stage Ten: Kaizen is infinite

Here we are, at the last stage – with this progression, it is vital that you understand that Kaizen is interminable. This is a process of learning and developing slowly, consistently, and constantly.

In many cases, it will reveal that life is a nonstop adventure, it isn't a goal – you should keep on moving through it. In the event that you rehearse the theory of constant change, at that point you will benefit as much as possible from this voyage we call life.

In the event that you need to keep on improving your life, you can't stay there in the loveseat and expect "Mr. Change" to thump on your front entryway. Change throughout everyday life, paying respect to who you might be, is something that will require some serious energy and work – it takes a ton of worthwhile effort.

Chapter 4

How to Create a Kaizen Culture at Home and at Work

The same amount of Kaizen, or the logic of nonstop change, is utilized to have all representatives at all organizational levels cooperate proactively, keeping in mind the end goal to accomplish normal, incremental enhancements to the assembly procedure, so that you can have all individuals from your family unit cooperating.

Try not to have one individual be the ruler, and instead have all relatives offer their proposals in general social gathering gatherings and work with the recommendations that can be accomplished. You will see that the mood of your home enhances and everybody will be significantly more joyful being a piece of a working procedure in an upbeat home.

Remember that Kaizen is part activity design and part logic. As an activity design, Kaizen is tied in with sorting out occasions that are centered around enhancing particular territories within the organization. Your house isn't an organization yet, and it can always utilize change where the family can live in amicability.

As a rationality, Kaizen is tied in with building a culture where all representatives are effectively occupied with recommending, and afterwards actualizing, changes to the organization.

In your home, once family members start helping each other with the typical every day assignments you will perceive what amount can be accomplished during the time it would take one relative to complete an undertaking. With kids who are of age to assist, it can improve things greatly to show them certain undertakings and enable them to comprehend why those things are important to achieve. You will see that even kids can be pleased with what they have realized and happy that you showed them these undertakings.

Kaizen works with nearby institutionalized work since institutionalized work deals with the prescribed procedures for a specific procedure, and Kaizen at that point discovers upgrades for these procedures.

You can make the utilization of a commonplace Kaizen occasion even in your own home. As a matter of importance, you should set objectives and see what needs enhancing in your home, and afterwards you should ensure that everybody comprehends why these objectives must be met.

At that point you can likewise build up an arrangement for development and actualize the changes. Once a specific undertaking has been refined, have a family meeting so you can get criticism from them regarding how fulfilled they are with what has been done and on the off chance that they comprehend why it must be finished. This will give them the motivation needed to do different assignments and to deeply consider what enhancements may be made.

It is fascinating to take note that Kaizen as an activity design is exactly what really creates Kaizen as a rationality. At that point, Kaizen is connected as an activity through nonstop and reliable fruitful Kaizen occasions to likewise show representatives, or as the case might be relatives to contemplate their work or assignments.

Actualize it without flaws and you can have a most agreeable home life.

With regards to the home and individual change, it is insightful to recollect that you ought not make progress toward enormous and brisk changes but rather with small and steady changes.

Remember that Kaizen is tied in with making small, incremental changes over a specific timeframe. At the point when these little changes are then aggravated they prompt outcomes that are more effective and more beneficial.

When implementing Kaizen into your life you should begin by separating your fantasies into smaller parts and choose what you need to accomplish every month, and at that point what to take a stab at every week, maybe even each day. It is vital that you focus assignments that are anything but difficult to finish and that will give you the best rewards first.

On the off chance that one of your objectives is to save money on foodstuffs and have healthier dinners, at that point begin with cut-out coupons, perusing names and discovering everything you can about the most advantageous dinners you can make. Begin by wiping out your kitchen from junk food, sugary beverages and snacks. Gradually, you will see the progressions you have been making, and soon you will see constant change in your way of life and your wellbeing. Make sure to roll out little and reasonable improvements consistently as opposed to making one monster jump which is certain to fall flat.

Make little undertakings which are sensible and feasible. Begin by going for long-haul changes that can compound throughout the years. Remember that the change needs to occur with you. So be resolved, never surrender, and you are certain to prevail in time. Try not to be restless on the grounds that all things and all improvements require some investment.

For them to succeed they should be nonstop and they should give you a chance to see the changes as time goes by. When you see yourself and your family driving a more joyful and more advantageous lifestyle then you realize that your underlying idea for eating better is working and that you are gradually accomplishing your objective for a vastly improved lifestyle.

At that point with the goal, you can likewise enhance different things and try out something new; test it out, and check whether it works, and in the event that it can likewise turn into a nonstop change. You are certain to have some disappointment and misses, however, adhere to the things that truly work. Along these lines you will again have an achievement, and you will see progressive and constant change over some undefined time frame.

Remember that with every choice you make, decide how your life will be extraordinary and better. In the event that it can be unique yet worse, take a stab at something different. Once your choices end up purposeful and thoroughly considered, then you will have a much clearer and better understanding of where you are running with the new changes and you are certain to end up with a win.

Kaizen culture in the work environment

Kaizen is a framework which requires association and investment from all representatives, from the forefront group to the upper administration and even the CEO. Everybody is urged to conceptualize and think of recommendations for development all the time. It is a constant action, done consistently.

Representatives from all levels of an organization proactively cooperate to accomplish constant, little, and incremental upgrades to the business forms. Along these lines, distinctive levels of encounters and aptitudes can be united to make capable methods for making changes in the organization's procedures.

Kaizen is a procedure, which if performed accurately, adapts the work environment, disposes of diligent work while empowering brilliant work, and rouses individuals to lead tests in light of their proposals, all while figuring out how to recognize and diminish squanders in the business methodologies. At the point when Kaizen is executed as an activity design through a progression of Kaizen occasions, it instructs representatives to contemplate their work. They are pushed into thinking how their present function can be additionally enhanced while keeping in mind the end goal to make more noteworthy progress.

Executing Kaizen in working environment

There are three phases for using Kaizen on any association.

Support cooperation – To guarantee dynamic investment from all representatives, it is vital that mindfulness about Kaizen is made. After the vital mindfulness, instructional courses are given, and give prizes to representatives on effective executions of ideas which are the aftereffects of these occasions. On such occasions, coordinated contributions of the administration is critical.

Preparing and Education – Appropriate preparation is required for officials to take in the substance of Kaizen. The administration level ought to completely comprehend Kaizen in an authoritative vision setting, which should be taken after vivaciously accomplishing the coveted business. They should likewise be instructed on how to be unprejudiced towards everybody and urge their representatives to effectively take an interest.

Quality level change – After preparations are complete, individuals should stay focussed on rolling out improvements towards change. They should take measures to begin rolling out incremental improvements towards accomplishing long haul objectives, such as enhancing productivity, procedures, and quality.

In associations where Kaizen is being actualized, straightforwardness between various levels of the association is exceptionally significant. Powerful correspondence should happen between every one of the levels of representatives. While workers are conceptualizing thoughts, it is essential that the administration likewise is associated with these sessions. The supervisor likewise ought to guarantee that their recommendations and thoughts are being followed up on promptly and not postponed by a week or month. Representatives ought to stay educated about different exercises going ahead in the group and how their thoughts are being functioned upon.

Individuals ought not feel that their thoughts have all gone to waste and are not being utilized. A positive outlook is the thing that will help in keeping Kaizen alive in the association.

Consequently, consistent use of Kaizen makes the enormous long haul an incentive by building up the way of life that is required for genuine constant change.

Chapter 5

Kaizen Methods & Benefits

As we have canvassed in the initial segment of this guide, The fundamental thought of Kaizen centers around enhancing procedures and items while in the meantime making the utilization of representative inventiveness to help in characterizing the way methods and frameworks can be moved forward.

Two of the general preferences of this theory incorporate expanded profitability and the capacity to keep up quality items and administrations. It is through cooperation that one benefits, not through independence. The Kaizen thought is extraordinary for making a work environment that values everyone.

Another preferred standpoint of Kaizen is the likelihood of making a tight-running business. When you begin rehearsing a technique like this, the majority of your workers will think in a "transport line" style and gain from each other while also sharing thoughts and recommendations for consistent change.

Kaizen enhances representative fulfillment by giving the specialists a chance to investigate the procedures and frameworks, as well as make proposals to facilitate change.

Getting together for group gatherings is an extraordinary path for workers to share their thoughts and think of more proposals in regards to enhancing quality.

Another great advantage of this sort of framework is expanded efficiency since laborers get more with the basic leadership process and they are anxious to see that their proposal work. It is likewise an awesome method to get new representatives when they see that everybody cooperates as a group.

By executing Kaizen in your business you can likewise enhance the wellbeing on the work floor.

When laborers perceive how this all functions, once something turns out badly they will be prepared to meet up and conceptualize thoughts on the best way to settle the circumstance as opposed to agonizing about it independently. It is similar to having an all around oiled machine in steady movement. It is useful for businesses since they can make sure that there will be less mishap-related injuries that can bring about diminished creation and workers requiring significant time off to deal with therapeutic crises.

Something else you can ensure is that if all of a sudden another undertaking rises due to continued progress any employee who definitely know how to do these errands will be prepared to demonstrate others how they are done. Thus, generation doesn't need to stop for a learning procedure, however, it can proceed as specialists learn as they go.

You can make sure that Kaizen will be an incredible benefit to your organization, your workers, and more importantly your organization's efficiency.

Chapter 6

Personal Kaizen

Above all else what you need to do is to begin your very own Kaizen and influence a rundown of the regions you to need to make strides. You can make you day more proficient by timing your exercises, and you can fill your heart with more joy by achieving the objectives you need to accomplish during the live long day.

Investigate what you invest the most energy in, for example; perusing emails, accepting telephone calls, or composing reports. Suppose that email sets aside the longest opportunity to sort. This is another thought of Kaizen – to begin with the lowliest of errands. You should seriously mull over presenting an envelope stream or make an inbox and an important box. Put aside time for the important mail first and do it a few times if there is a great deal. At that point leave the normal inbox to get out when you have achieved different undertakings first.

What you need to do is to externalize considerations and "free" yourself for the undertakings that must be proficient in one working day. Regardless of whether you put aside different assignments for the next day you will have the fulfillment that what must be done was finished.

In some cases, when you are finished with the vital assignments you may investigate the less critical ones and maybe some of them can be joined into one major errand which makes it simpler to deal with and requires less time.

Kaizen centers around disposing of waste. In an organization it is imperative to have representatives set up instrument stations so everything is effortlessly within reach and no time is squandered searching for specific things. By removing steps that dawdle, efficiency can be significantly increased.

Another Kaizen rule is institutionalization when you consider what the accepted procedures are and do this before they are put into movement.

When you prepare yourself by imagining these practices, you can have them actualized naturally. When you perceive how these practices function then you can consider if any of them require any change and work on that straightaway.

It can be a smart thought to embrace one new practice every month. Sooner or later you will see which of these practices end up obsolete and proceed onward to another. Ensure that you monitor them and soon you will see that as stunning as it appears there might even be some time every day to kick back and think about the working procedure and recover.

You need to have everything running easily which significantly calms the brain, and after that you can focus on the more troublesome assignments which may be causing a few issues.

Remember that Kaizen is a framework for presenting process enhancements, and the most critical thing is to utilize these frameworks so that you can make your life substantially less demanding.

You can get more work done from cheerful and fulfilled representatives than from troubled and overworked representatives. When representatives are additionally helping each other to comprehend certain procedures and everybody is learning as they go you can ensure that creation doesn't stop. This will likewise free you up to focus on the undertakings that are most important to you.

Conclusion

Congrats on making it to the end of this guide on the rationality of Kaizen!

You might be amazed to realize that the lion's share of individuals who begin perusing a book never finish it. On the off chance that you've made it this far, you have certainly been inspired by Kaizen and every one of the advantages that it brings to the table.

Here are some manners by which you can utilize the Kaizen rationality to accomplish your definitive goals.

Inspire yourself

There is a maxim, "the psyche is solid, yet the tissue is frail!" Start by partnering with individuals who have an inspirational outlook, individuals who can give you word of wisdoms and great information.

Utilize what you have learned from your missteps. You can utilize visual jolts, similar to a notice demonstrating a place, or brandishing an occasion that you are intent on visiting later. You can likewise utilize a timetable and stamp off the days to demonstrate how you are advancing towards your objective.

I have utilized this specific strategy effectively myself. On the off chance that I had not utilized this technique, I seriously doubt that I would have accomplished my life-long desires.

Anticipating obstacles

We as a whole realize that it is exceptionally hard to dispose of old propensities and in the meantime, new propensities are hard to keep up. It is tied in with keeping solid!

It is vital that we understand that we will slip once in a while and that we have an arrangement set up to expect issues that may happen. Such is reality for you and we must be ready for a few things not to go as planned.

Reinforce any potential weaknesses in your plan

You have to figure out how to transform pardons into circumstances. This will make you more grounded. There are numerous things in life that set us up for disappointment. Money related issues, social connections, transport and a horde of other different things. These keep us from achieving our goals on the off chance that we enable them to. Attempt and transform them into qualities and think of choices instead of totally surrendering.

Be YOUR best self

Kaizen's philosophy is to persuade every individual to be as well as can be expected by taking baby steps.

Quit comparing yourself with others. Simply be as well as can be expected at all that you do. Get things done in your time, enhancing yourself step by step. Have that psychological quality to stick it out when you need to stop and realize that towards the day's end, you have given your all to achieving your objective.

www.ingramcontent.com/pod-product-compliance
Lightning Source LLC
Chambersburg PA
CBHW030036230526
45472CB00002B/546